My First Book about Cheetahs

Amazing Animal Books
Children's Picture Books

By Molly Davidson

Mendon Cottage Books
JD-Biz Corp Publishing

Download Free Books!
http://MendonCottageBooks.com

Read More Amazing Animal Books

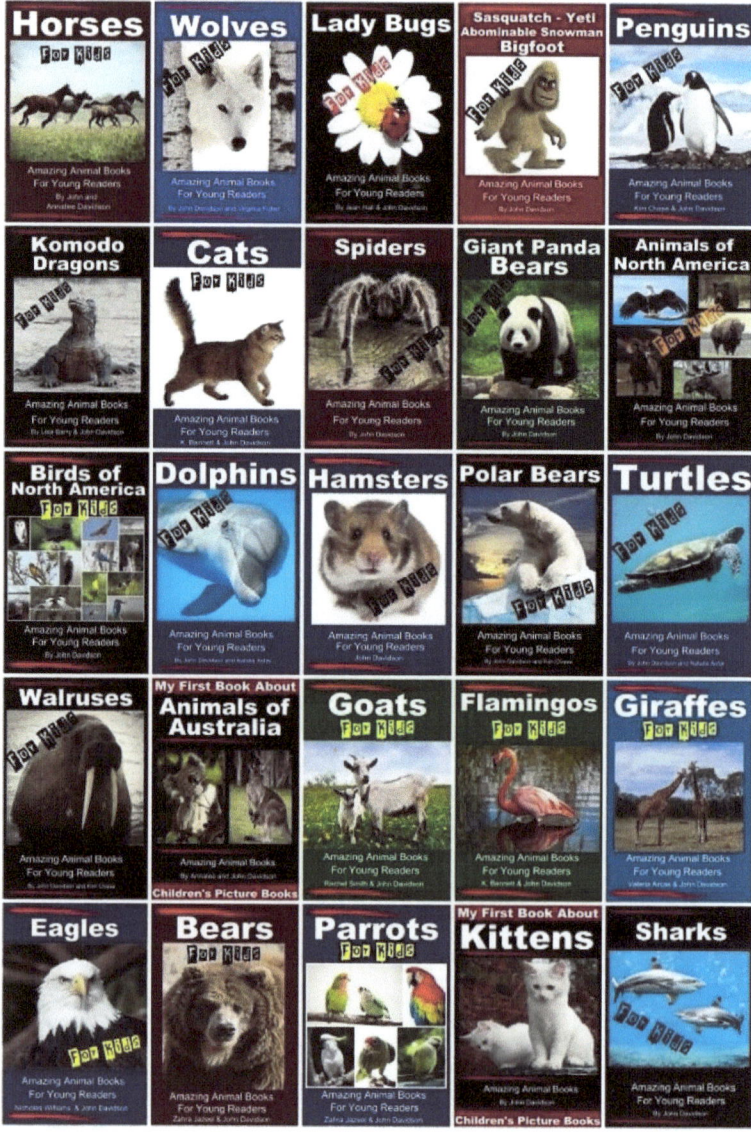

Purchase at Amazon.com

Table of Contents

Introduction

Cheetahs are the fastest land animal alive.

They live mostly in Africa, and a few in Iran .Many use to live in Asia, but the growing number of people pushed them out of their habitat.

Let's learn more about this amazing animal, the cheetah.

What is a cheetah?

A cheetah is one of the big cats, along with lions, tigers, jaguars, and leopards.

A cheetah mother and her cub

Cheetahs are not even close to as strong as the other big cats.

They are skinny and built for speed.

They are not meant for running long distances, short quick bursts is what cheetahs do best.

They are also very swift and can change directions and speeds in split seconds.

Cheetahs have rough golden fur that is covered in black spots.

They have white fur on their bellies and the end of their tail.

Cheetahs also have black rings around their eyes, which helps them see without getting blinded by the sun, since the color black does not reflect light.

To help them run faster, cheetahs have large nose holes, called nostrils, which help them breathe in more oxygen.

They will use their tail to steer and to turn.

Cheetahs also have semi-retractable claws, which means they can be all the out, half out, or all the way in. This helps them grip the ground when needed.

They cannot roar like the other big cats, cheetahs purr instead.

How do cheetahs act?

Boy and girl cheetahs act very differently, even though they look the same.

Boys like to live in groups and hang out together, usually with their brothers.

They also have territories that they protect until death, if another boy cheetah tries to come in, they will kill it without even thinking.

Girls live by themselves or with their cubs until they are old enough to survive alone, about a year.

They live in large areas called home ranges, which overlap many of the boys territories, so they can be found during mating season.

Mothers will make a high chirping sound when looking for her cubs.

Cheetahs also make a sound called churring, which is a mixture of chirping and growling. This is usually an invitation to talk or hang out together.

They will growl and spit at each other, this usually means there is danger.

Cheetah cubs will purr to show they are happy.

What do Cheetahs eat?

Cheetahs are a carnivore, which means a meat eater.

Antelope is what they hunt and eat the most.

They will also hunt fox, ostriches, warthogs, zebras, and a few other animals.

Cheetahs use their excellent eye-sight to hunt; they will sneak up really close to their prey, then run fast to catch it.

If a cheetah cannot kill its prey within a minute, it will stop chasing it, and will save its energy for something easier.

They try to run and trip their prey, and then dig their sharp teeth into the neck, killing the animal.

Cheetahs kill about half they prey they go after.

If another animal comes to take their kill, cheetahs will not fight, they will just leave.

They cannot risk getting hurt, and then they will not be able to run and catch more food.

Many cheetahs that get hurt die of hunger because they cannot go catch food for themselves.

Cheetah Babies

Mothers will usually have 6 cubs, but most of those do not survive their first year.

Many predators like to eat cheetah cubs, like lion and African wild dogs.

Cubs have a bunch of bluish fur on the top of their heads, called a mantle.

Scientists believe cubs have a mantle to protect themselves from predators; it makes them look like a honey badger, which is a mean animal that no one wants to mess with.

What kinds of cheetahs are there?

A cheetah in Kenya, Africa

There are five subspecies of the cheetah, which means it is a cheetah, but a specific type.

First, is the South African cheetah, which is an endangered species.

Next is the Tanzanian cheetah, which lives throughout the African grasslands.

Third is the Sudan cheetah, which is very similar to the South African cheetah. There are only about 2,000 left in the wild.

A cheetah in the African bush

The Northwest African cheetah is the smallest of the cheetahs. It is highly endangered, with only about 250 left in the wild.

The last species of cheetah is the Asiatic cheetah, which can now only be found in national parks in Iran. It is the only cheetah to live outside of Africa and to have a thick, woolly, winter coat.

An Asiatic Cheetah

Behnam Ghorbani © <u>Wikimedia Commons</u>

The history of cheetahs and humans

A cheetah within an enclosure in Namibia, Africa

Humans have been taming cheetahs for hundreds
years. They are easier to tame than other big cats,
because they will just run away instead of harming a
human.

Ancient Egyptians trained cheetahs to help in hunts.
They would blindfold them until the hunting dogs

had chased out the prey, then the cheetahs would be released to go kill.

Genghis Khan, a Mongolian conqueror, and King Charlemagne of France had cheetahs as pets.

In Persia and India, princes wanted as many cheetahs as they could get to show how powerful and wealthy they were.

Cheetahs are now illegal to have as a pet and are only kept in zoos. They do not do very well there, they are too nervous since it is not their natural habitat.

Cheetahs and conservation

Cheetahs are endangered, but there are people out there helping to protect them.

A cheetah mother and her two young cubs

One problem scientists are finding is that cheetahs are too much the same, so any disease kills all cheetahs; none of them are protected from it.

A major problem is humans are taking over their territory, so they have nowhere to live.

Many farmers are hurting or killing cheetahs to protect their livestock, but the cheetahs are just hungry and have nowhere else to go.

The last issue is the illegal selling of baby cheetahs, and cheetah fur.

Morphs and other differences among cheetahs

Morphs are when there's a different kind of coat or fur appearance than normal, it's just a rare version of a cheetah.

A king cheetah

One type of cheetah morph is the king cheetah, it is a little bigger and powerful. It also has stripes and patches of black fur instead of dots.

Other morph cheetahs can be all black, chinchillism (grayish), and albino (all white).

Conclusion

Cheetahs are such amazing animals; I hope we can all do our part to help keep them around for many more years to come.

Publisher

JD-Biz Corp

P O Box 374

Mendon, Utah 84325

http://www.jd-biz.com/

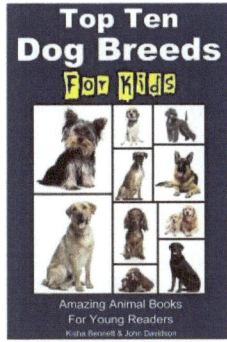
Top Ten Dog Breeds For Kids
Amazing Animal Books For Young Readers
Kisha Bennett & John Davidson

German Shepherds
Dog Books for Kids
K. Bennett

Bulldogs
Dog Books for Kids
K. Bennett

Dachshund
Dog Books for Kids
K. Bennett

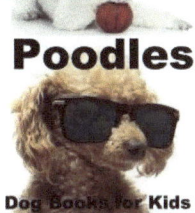
Poodles
Dog Books for Kids
K. Bennett

Labrador Retrievers
Dog Books for Kids
K. Bennett

Rottweilers
Dog Books for Kids
K. Bennett

Boxers
Dog Books for Kids
K. Bennett

Golden Retrievers
Dog Books for Kids
K. Bennett

Puppies
Dog Books For Kids
Amazing Animal Books
By John Davidson

Beagles

Dog Books for Kids
K. Bennett

Yorkshire Terriers
Dog Books for Kids
K. Bennett

Dogs
Top Ten Dog Breeds For Kids
Amazing Animal Books For Young Readers
Zahra Jazeel & John Davidson

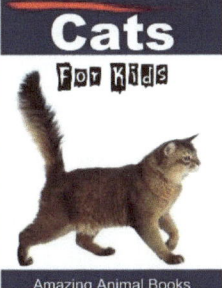
Cats
For Kids
Amazing Animal Books For Young Readers
K. Bennett & John Davidson

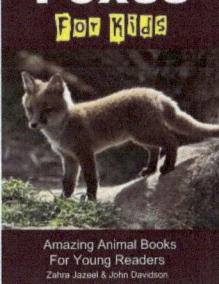
Foxes
For Kids
Amazing Animal Books For Young Readers
Zahra Jazeel & John Davidson

Wolves
For Kids
Amazing Animal Books For Young Readers
By John Davidson and Virginia Fidler

Our books are available at

1. Amazon.com

2. Barnes and Noble

3. Itunes

4. Kobo

5. Smashwords

6. Google Play Books

Download Free Books!
http://MendonCottageBooks.com